THE SOUP COOKBOOK

Books in the Penguin Pocket Series

THE AUSTRALIAN CALORIE COUNTER
THE AUSTRALIAN EASY SPELLER
AUSTRALIAN GARDENING CALENDAR
CASSEROLES FOR FAMILY AND FRIENDS
CHAIRING AND RUNNING MEETINGS
CHESS MADE EASY
CHOOSING A NAME FOR YOUR BABY
CHOOSING AUSTRALIAN WINES
THE COMPACT GUIDE TO WRITING LETTERS
FAMILY FIRST AID
GABRIEL GATÉ'S FAST PASTA
GABRIEL GATÉ'S FAVOURITE FAST RECIPES
GABRIEL GATÉ'S ONE-DISH DINNERS
GOOD FOOD FOR BABIES AND TODDLERS
HOW TO MAKE OVER 200 COCKTAILS
HOW TO PLAY MAH JONG
JULIE STAFFORD'S FAT, FIBRE & ENERGY COUNTER
JULIE STAFFORD'S JUICING BOOK
MICROWAVE MEALS IN MINUTES
MICROWAVE TIPS AND TECHNIQUES
THE PENGUIN BOOK OF ETIQUETTE
THE PENGUIN POCKET BOOK OF QUOTATIONS
PLAYING CASINO GAMES TO WIN
THE POCKET AUSSIE FACT BOOK
THE POCKET MUFFIN BOOK
THE POCKET WOK COOKBOOK
THE POCKET SOUP COOKBOOK
REMOVING STAINS
SPEAKING IN PUBLIC
TRAINING YOUR MEMORY
USING YOUR NOODLES
WEDDING ETIQUETTE
YOUR NEW BABY

THE POCKET SOUP COOKBOOK

SYD PEMBERTON

PENGUIN BOOKS

Penguin Books Australia Ltd
487 Maroondah Highway, PO Box 257
Ringwood, Victoria 3134, Australia
Penguin Books Ltd
Harmondsworth, Middlesex, England
Penguin Putnam Inc.
375 Hudson Street, New York, New York 10014, USA
Penguin Books Canada Limited
10 Alcorn Avenue, Toronto, Ontario, Canada M4V 3B2
Penguin Books (NZ) Ltd
Cnr Rosedale and Airborne Roads, Albany, Auckland, New Zealand
Penguin Books (South Africa) (Pty) Ltd
24 Sturdee Avenue, Rosebank, Johannesburg 2196, South Africa
Penguin Books India (P) Ltd
11, Community Centre, Panchsheel Park, New Delhi 110 017, India

First published by Penguin Books Australia Ltd 2001

3 5 7 9 10 8 6 4 2

Copyright © Penguin Books Australia Ltd 2001

All rights reserved. Without limiting the rights under copyright reserved above, no part of this publication may be reproduced, stored in or introduced into a retrieval system, or transmitted, in any form or by any means (electronic, mechanical, photocopying, recording or otherwise), without the prior written permission of both the copyright owner and the above publisher of this book.

Design by Melissa Fraser, Penguin Design Studio
Cover photograph by Julie Anne Renouf
Food styling and preparation by Maureen McKeon
Typeset in 10 pt Apollo by Post Pre-press Group, Brisbane, Queensland
Printed and bound in Australia by McPherson's Printing Group, Maryborough, Victoria

National Library of Australia
Cataloguing-in-Publication data:

Pemberton, Syd.
The pocket soup cookbook.

Includes index.
ISBN 0 14 028243 2.

1. Soups. I. Title.

641.813

www.penguin.com.au

Cover image shows Pear, Pea and Watercress Soup (page 33).

contents

introduction

Soup is a simple staple dish that has evolved over hundreds of thousands of years.

It all began with a few bones and vegetables thrown into a primitive pot with some water and wild herbs, which were then cooked up to produce a tasty, warming dish. Specialities developed in regions all over the world as cooks used the ingredients that were available to them. Even today soup is still the sort of dish where anything goes. It is now truly international fare, but remains true to its original form – simple to make and full of flavour.

Here is a collection of recipes celebrating the wide range of ingredients, flavours and textures that can be used to make soup. I have divided the book into several broad categories. To cater for people's dietary needs and preferences, the soups are divided into Smooth Creamy Soups, Hearty Vegetable Soups, Seafood Soups and Warming Winter Soups (where you will find recipes that include meat) and Chilled Summer Soups. But of course any soup can be a light luncheon, a mouth-watering starter or a whole meal in a bowl, depending on the size of the helping or the accompaniment you serve with it.

I took great pleasure in compiling these recipes, as I sourced ingredients from the vegetable garden and market, the refrigerator and the pantry. The result is a selection of flavoursome, easy-to-make specialties for you to enjoy.

Serves – You will find that most recipes in this book will serve four to six people, but some of the more hearty soups will make six to eight portions. It is always a good idea to make extra soup as the flavours become more intense on the second and third days.

Storage – Soup is the perfect fare for busy people because it stores well. Most vegetable-based soups will keep in the refrigerator for three to four days. Soups containing meat, seafood and poultry can be stored for two to three days. Keep in an airtight container. When freezing soups, fill the container two-thirds full to allow for expansion of the liquid. Label and date the containers.

for added flavour and texture

Add a few extra ingredients to a simple soup to turn it into the most exotic dish. Depending on just how much extra flavour and texture are required, you can experiment with these suggested garnishes and accompaniments.

Buttermilk makes a delicious low-fat alternative to full-fat cream when added to cold soups (it will curdle if added to hot liquids).

Crème fraîche is an excellent garnish or thickener as it does not curdle when added to hot soups. Nor does it curdle when boiled. It is made from fresh or sour cream and buttermilk, and can be used instead of full-fat cream. You can make your own crème fraîche by combining 500 ml cream with 250 ml buttermilk in a saucepan and heating until just warm (24°C). Remove to a bowl. Cover with clingwrap, leaving a small gap for air. Stand at room temperature overnight or until thickened. Chill until ready to use.

Croutes are thin slices of French bread brushed with olive oil and baked in a preheated oven (180°C) for 8–10 minutes until crisp and brown. Rub garlic or other seasonings into the bread before baking for a stronger flavour. Float whole croutes on top of the soup before serving.

Croutons make a delicious garnish for all types of soups. Trim crusts off sliced bread and cut into small cubes. Bake on a lightly oiled baking tray in a preheated oven (180°C) for 4–8 minutes or until crisp and just browned. Alternatively, heat 3 tablespoons light olive oil in a frying pan and toss in bread cubes. Cook until crisp and brown. Remove and drain on kitchen paper. Use flavoured oils to produce a variety of croutons or sprinkle seasonings or fresh herbs over croutons before adding to the soup.

Herbs and spices are ideal garnishes for soups. Fresh herbs such as shredded kaffir lime leaves, chervil, Vietnamese mint, Thai basil and parsley each add special flavours. A pinch of black sesame seeds, dry-roasted cumin seeds, fennel seeds or freshly grated nutmeg can add spicy or crunchy elements.

Pita bread toast is a simpler version of Melba toast. Cut oval pita pocket bread into quarters, open up and separate into triangles. Preheat the oven to 220°C. Lightly brush pita bread with oil and bake for 8–10 minutes until crisp and brown. Sprinkle over sesame seeds, lemon pepper seasoning or a little chopped garlic for special soups.

Sour cream is a thick cream with a sour, sharp taste. Made from full cream, it is delicious as a garnish in hot or cold soups. It will curdle if added to very hot liquids and then boiled, so stir it into the soup off the heat just before serving.

Thickeners can help bind solid ingredients together, stopping them from sinking to the bottom. There are numerous ideas for thickeners and it really depends on the sort of soup you are making.

- Mix together equal amounts of butter and flour to form a thick paste, then drop the paste into the soup in pea-sized amounts.
- Peel and grate 1 medium-sized floury potato. Add to soup at the same time as adding stock.
- Combine 2 tablespoons cornflour, rice flour, potato flour or arrowroot with ¼ cup soup liquid to make a smooth paste. Add to soup and simmer for the last 5 minutes before serving.
- Beat 2 egg yolks and slowly whisk into soup off the heat. Return soup to heat and simmer for 5 minutes before serving. Used in delicate soups, this method will add flavour and colour.

Yoghurt (plain) is an excellent substitute for cream in soups. It may curdle if boiled, therefore it is best to stir it into the soup just before serving.

Unusual garnishes and accompaniments turn a good soup into a sensational soup. Try any of the following for a crunchy, nutty, flavoursome dish: pappadums, rice crackers, prawn crackers, tortilla chips, crispy fried onions, beetroot or parsnip chips, puff pastry shapes, spicy fruit chutney, chopped nuts, toasted coconut.

kitchen essentials

As with any cooking process, you will need some good basic equipment. It is worth investing in a 4–5 litre heavy-based saucepan with a lid. This is suitable for all soup recipes. You will also need a fine sieve. Use the sieve to strain the liquid back into the saucepan, pushing through most of the contents. This ensures that there are no lumps in the soup. You will need either an electric blender or food processor, a hand-held blender or a food mill. The texture of a soup will vary according to the equipment used.

Potato-based soups are best puréed in a blender or food mill as a food processor tends to purée them into a starchy pulp. It is always best to cool the soup a little first before blending. Make sure that you do not overfill the blender or food processor and the lid is firmly attached. Season to taste after you have blended the soup.

stocks

The most important basic ingredient for a delicious soup is a full-flavoured stock. Stocks are easy to make and can be stored in the freezer ready to use.

The stock specified in each recipe is my preferred one, but in many recipes one stock can be substituted for another; for example, a vegetable stock can be used instead of a meat stock. However, usually a fish stock should only be used for a fish soup.

Stock cubes, pastes and powders are a good standby, but they can be quite salty so you may need to adjust the amount of extra salt you add to the soup.

Beef Stock

2 kg beef bones
2 onions, quartered
2 carrots, peeled and coarsely chopped
2 sticks celery, coarsely chopped
4 cloves garlic, crushed
4 litres water
10 black peppercorns
4 sprigs parsley
4 bay leaves

Preheat oven to 220°C. Place beef bones in a shallow roasting tin and roast for 40 minutes, turning occasionally. Add vegetables and cook for 15–20 minutes. Remove from oven and, using a slotted spoon to drain off any excess fat, place bones and vegetables in a large saucepan.

Pour in water and add herbs and spices. Bring to the boil and then simmer over a low heat for 4–5 hours, skimming the top from time to time. Remove from heat and strain stock. Cool before refrigerating. When cold, remove any fat that has settled on the top. Freeze or use as required.

Chicken Stock

1 kg chicken bones, skin removed (include a few chicken feet)
4 stalks celery, roughly chopped
2 carrots, peeled and coarsely chopped

2 onions, coarsely chopped
1 leek, washed and chopped
8 black peppercorns
1 sprig each parsley, thyme, bay leaves
2 litres water

Place all ingredients in a large saucepan, cover and bring to boil. Remove lid and simmer for about 1 hour, skimming the top with a spoon frequently to remove any sludge. Check seasoning and continue cooking for a further hour.

Remove from heat and strain. Cool before refrigerating. When cold, remove any fat that has settled on the top. Freeze or use as required.

Fish Stock

1 kg white-fish bones and heads
1 onion, sliced into rings
1 stalk celery, sliced
1 sprig each parsley and thyme
2 bay leaves
1 star anise
6 black peppercorns
250 ml white wine
1 strip lemon peel
1.25 litres water

Wash the fish heads and bones under cold running water. Cut into 4–5 pieces. Place all ingredients in a large saucepan and slowly bring to the boil. Simmer for 20 minutes, skimming off any surface sludge. Remove from heat and strain into a bowl, then cool and refrigerate. Freeze or use as required.

A quick fish stock can also be made from prawn, lobster or crab shells. Use the same ingredients as for fish stock, but use shells instead of fish bones.

Vegetable Stock

2 large potatoes, scrubbed and coarsely chopped
2 large carrots, peeled and sliced
1 large onion, quartered
2 leeks, washed and sliced
1 stalk celery, chopped
1 apple, quartered
1 bay leaf
12 peppercorns
1 tablespoon yeast extract
2 litres water

Place all ingredients in a large saucepan and bring to the boil. Simmer, uncovered, for 45 minutes, then strain. Cool and store in the refrigerator until ready to use or freeze.

smooth creamy soups

Tomato and Orange Soup

2 tablespoons light olive oil
1 large onion, finely chopped
2 cloves garlic, finely chopped
1 kg ripe tomatoes, roughly chopped
salt and freshly ground black pepper
1 bay leaf
4 cups chicken or vegetable stock
zest and juice of 1 orange
2 tablespoons freshly chopped parsley

In a saucepan heat oil and add onion and garlic. Cook over a gentle heat until soft. Add tomato, salt and pepper and bay leaf and pour in stock. Slowly bring to the boil and cook, covered, for 15–20 minutes until tomato is soft. Remove from heat, remove bay leaf and cool a little.

Place in a blender or food processor and purée until smooth. Sieve back into the saucepan and add orange zest and juice. Gently reheat and check seasoning. Ladle into bowls and garnish with parsley.

Fresh Tomato Soup

25 g butter
1 onion, finely chopped
2 cloves garlic, crushed
1 potato, peeled and thinly sliced
500 g ripe tomatoes, roughly chopped
1 bay leaf
2 tablespoons tomato paste
4 cups vegetable stock
salt and freshly ground black pepper
½ cup crème fraîche
1 tablespoon finely chopped fresh parsley

In a saucepan melt butter and add onion and garlic. Cook over a gentle heat until soft. Add potato, tomato, bay leaf, tomato paste and stock. Bring to the boil and simmer, covered, for about 20 minutes until potato is tender. Remove from heat and cool a little.

Place in a blender or food processor and purée until smooth. Return to the saucepan and gently reheat. Stir in crème fraîche. Ladle into bowls and garnish with parsley.

Carrot and Fresh Ginger Soup

25 g butter
¼ teaspoon curry powder
1 large onion, finely chopped
¼ cup fresh ginger, peeled and finely chopped
400 g carrots, peeled and thinly sliced
4 cups chicken or vegetable stock
2 tablespoons lemon juice
salt and freshly ground black pepper
2 tablespoons finely chopped fresh parsley

In a saucepan melt butter and add curry powder, onion and ginger. Cook until onion is soft. Add carrot and cook, covered, for 20 minutes, stirring from time to time. Pour in stock and bring to the boil. Simmer for 15 minutes or until carrot is tender. Remove from heat and cool a little.

Place in a blender or food processor and purée until smooth. Return to the saucepan and gently reheat. Stir in lemon juice and season to taste. Ladle into bowls and top with parsley.

Carrot, Sweet Potato and Peanut Butter Soup

1 tablespoon light olive oil
1 onion, finely chopped
½ teaspoon finely grated fresh ginger
2 cloves garlic, crushed
¼ teaspoon cayenne pepper
2 carrots, peeled and finely chopped
2 sweet potatoes, peeled and thinly sliced
4 cups chicken or vegetable stock
½ cup smooth peanut butter
2 tomatoes, roughly chopped
1 tablespoon finely chopped fresh chives

In a saucepan heat oil and add onion, ginger, garlic, cayenne pepper and carrot. Cook over a gentle heat for 3–4 minutes. Add potato and pour in stock. Slowly bring to the boil and simmer for about 15 minutes or until vegetables are tender. Remove from heat and cool a little.

Place in a blender or food processor and purée until smooth. Return to the saucepan and gently reheat. Add peanut butter, stirring until smooth. Ladle soup into bowls and garnish with chopped tomato and chives.

Red Pepper Soup with Coriander Pesto

2 large red peppers
1 tablespoon olive oil
1 small onion, finely chopped
2 cloves garlic, finely chopped
400 g tinned plum tomatoes
4 cups vegetable stock
1 teaspoon lemon zest
2–3 tablespoons lemon juice
2 teaspoons sugar
salt and freshly ground black pepper

Coriander Pesto
1 bunch fresh coriander, leaves trimmed and stems discarded
1 bunch parsley, leaves trimmed and stems discarded
2 cloves garlic, crushed
60 g roasted cashew nuts
60 g freshly grated parmesan cheese
3–4 tablespoons olive oil

To make coriander pesto, blend first five ingredients in a food processor, then gradually add oil until a smooth, creamy sauce forms.

Cut peppers in half and remove pith and seeds. Grill until skins are blistered and blackened. Remove to a plastic bag and cool for 5 minutes. When cool, remove skins and finely chop flesh.

In a saucepan heat oil and add onion and garlic. Cook over a gentle heat for 3–4 minutes. Add pepper, tomato and stock. Bring to the boil and simmer for 15–20 minutes. Remove from heat and cool a little. Add lemon zest and juice, sugar and salt and pepper.

Place in a food processor or blender and purée until smooth. Check seasoning and return to the saucepan. Ladle into soup bowls and garnish with coriander pesto.

Broccoli Soup with Ricotta

2 tablespoons canola oil
1 large onion, thinly sliced
1 clove garlic, finely chopped
1 carrot, peeled and thinly sliced
1 stalk celery, finely chopped
4 cups chicken stock
600 g broccoli, trimmed into small florets
pinch of cayenne pepper
salt
½ cup ricotta cheese

In a saucepan heat oil and add onion, garlic, carrot and celery. Cook over a gentle heat until soft. Pour in stock and bring to the boil. Add broccoli and cook until tender. Remove from heat and cool a little.

Place in a blender or food processor and purée until smooth. Return to the saucepan and gently reheat. Season to taste with cayenne pepper and salt. Ladle into bowls and spoon in a couple of dollops of ricotta.

Broccoli Stalk Soup

20 g butter
2 leeks, washed and thinly sliced
2 cloves garlic, finely chopped
1 kg broccoli stalks, trimmed and thinly sliced
1 large potato, peeled and thinly sliced
3 cups chicken or vegetable stock
salt and freshly ground black pepper
200 ml crème fraîche
1 cup croutons
½ teaspoon lemon pepper seasoning

In a saucepan melt butter and add leek and garlic. Cook over a gentle heat until soft. Add broccoli stalks and potato and pour in stock. Slowly bring to the boil and cook, covered, for 15–20 minutes until vegetables are tender. Remove from heat and cool a little.

Place in a blender or food processor and purée until smooth. Return to the saucepan and gently reheat. Stir in crème fraîche. Season to taste. Ladle into bowls, toss a few croutons over the top and sprinkle with a little lemon pepper seasoning.

Cauliflower Cheese and Seeded Mustard Soup

?

25 g butter
1 onion, finely chopped
2 cloves garlic, crushed
3 cups vegetable stock
1 medium cauliflower, cut into small florets
1 large potato, peeled and thinly sliced
1 heaped tablespoon coarse-grain mustard
½ cup crème fraîche or cream
salt and freshly ground black pepper
2 cups croutons
¼ cup grated Swiss cheese

In a saucepan melt butter and add onion and garlic. Cook over a gentle heat until soft. Add potato and cauliflower and pour in stock. Slowly bring to the boil and cook, covered, for 15–20 minutes until vegetables are tender. Remove from heat and cool a little.

Place in a blender or food processor and purée until smooth. Return to the saucepan and gently reheat. Stir in mustard and crème fraîche. Season to taste. Ladle into bowls, toss a few croutons over the top and sprinkle with a little cheese.

Button Mushroom Soup

50 g butter
250 g white button mushrooms, wiped clean and roughly chopped
1 onion, finely chopped
25 g plain flour
4 cups chicken stock
½ cup medium sherry
150 ml milk
salt and freshly ground black pepper
½ cup herbed croutons

In a saucepan melt butter and add mushroom and onion. Cook over a low heat for 10 minutes until soft. Stir in flour and cook for 1–2 minutes. Stir in stock a little at a time and slowly bring to the boil. Simmer for 15 minutes, then remove from heat and cool a little.

Place in a blender or food processor and purée until smooth. Return to the saucepan and stir in sherry. Gently cook for 5 minutes. Stir in milk and season to taste. Ladle into bowls and garnish with croutons.

Indian Spiced Field Mushroom Soup

2 tablespoons olive oil
1 onion, finely chopped
1 carrot, finely chopped
2 sticks celery, finely chopped
2 cloves garlic, crushed
½ teaspoon turmeric
¼ teaspoon cayenne pepper
1 teaspoon ground cumin
2 teaspoons crushed cardamom seeds
2 bay leaves
500 g large, flat field mushrooms, peeled,
stalks removed and roughly chopped
4 cups chicken or vegetable stock
2 tablespoons finely chopped fresh coriander
½ cup creamy yoghurt
8 cooked pappadums

In a large saucepan heat oil and add onion, carrot, celery, garlic and spices. Cook over a gentle heat for 4–5 minutes until soft. Add mushrooms and cook for 6–8 minutes, stirring occasionally. Pour in stock and bring to the boil. Simmer for 15 minutes until mushrooms are cooked. Remove from heat and cool a little. Remove bay leaves.

Place in a blender or food processor and purée until smooth. Return to the saucepan and stir in coriander. Ladle soup into bowls and serve with a dollop of creamy yoghurt and garnish with broken pappadums.

Mushroom and Almond Soup

25 g butter
1 onion, finely chopped
2 cloves garlic, crushed
½ teaspoon dried thyme
250 g mushrooms, wiped clean and
roughly chopped
3 cups vegetable stock
1 cup milk
½ cup roasted, chopped almonds
salt and freshly ground black pepper
1 tablespoon almond flakes

In a saucepan melt butter and add onion and garlic. Cook over a gentle heat until soft. Add thyme and mushrooms and cook for 3–4 minutes. Add stock and bring to the boil. Simmer, covered, for about 20 minutes. Stir in milk and almonds. Remove from heat and cool a little.

Place in a blender or food processor and purée until smooth. Return to the saucepan and gently reheat. Season to taste. Ladle into bowls and garnish with almond flakes.

Apple, Pecan and Blue Cheese Soup

20 g butter
1 small onion, finely chopped
2 sticks celery, finely chopped
4 Granny Smith apples, peeled, cored and thinly sliced
4 cups chicken stock
150 g blue cheese
½ cup cream
½ cup white wine
½ cup finely chopped pecans
salt and freshly ground black pepper
2 tablespoons finely chopped fresh chives

In a saucepan heat butter and add onion, celery and apple. Cook over a gentle heat until soft. Add stock and bring to the boil. Simmer for 20 minutes. Remove from heat and cool a little.

Place in a blender or food processor with blue cheese and purée. Return to the saucepan and stir in cream, white wine and pecans. Season to taste. Gently reheat, then ladle into bowls and garnish with chives.

Curried Apple and Celery Soup

25 g butter
2 onions, finely chopped
2 sticks celery, finely chopped
2 large Granny Smith apples, peeled, cored and finely chopped
2 tablespoons flour
2 tablespoons curry powder
4 cups chicken stock
salt and freshly ground black pepper
½ cup yoghurt
1 tablespoon finely chopped fresh chives

In a large saucepan melt butter and add onion, celery and apple. Cook for 3–4 minutes, then stir in flour and curry powder. Cook for 2 minutes, then slowly pour in stock. Slowly bring to the boil and simmer, uncovered, for 20 minutes until vegetables are tender. Remove from heat and cool a little.

Place in a blender or food processor and purée until smooth. Return to the saucepan and gently reheat. Season to taste. Ladle into bowls and garnish with a little yoghurt and chopped chives.

Celery and Chestnut Soup

25 g butter
1 onion, finely chopped
2 cloves garlic, crushed
1 carrot, peeled and finely chopped
4 sticks celery, finely chopped
1 bay leaf
300 g canned whole chestnuts, rinsed and drained
1 potato, peeled and thinly sliced
3 cups chicken stock
2 tablespoons lemon juice
4 tablespoons light sour cream
2 tablespoons finely chopped fresh chives

In a saucepan melt butter and add onion and garlic. Cook over a gentle heat until soft. Add carrot, celery and bay leaf and cook for 3–4 minutes. Add chestnuts, potato and stock and bring to the boil. Simmer, covered, until chestnuts and potato are tender, about 20 minutes. Remove from heat and cool a little.

Place in a blender or food processor and purée until smooth. Return to the saucepan and gently reheat. Season to taste. Ladle into bowls and garnish with sour cream and chives.

Cream of Fennel Soup

2 tablespoons light olive oil
2 bulbs fennel, trimmed and finely chopped
1 large onion, finely chopped
salt and freshly ground black pepper
½ teaspoon fennel seeds
4 cups chicken stock
½ cup crème fraîche
1 cup garlic croutons

In a saucepan heat oil and add onion and fennel. Cook over a gentle heat for 8–10 minutes, stirring occasionally. Season to taste and add fennel seeds. Pour in stock and bring to the boil. Simmer, covered, until fennel is tender. Remove from heat and cool a little.

Place in a blender or food processor and purée until smooth. Return to the saucepan and gently reheat. Check seasoning. Stir in crème fraîche just before serving. Garnish with croutons.

Celeriac, Leek and Apple Soup

25 g butter
2 leeks, washed and roughly chopped
1 celeriac head, peeled and roughly chopped (approximately 500 g)
2 Granny Smith apples, peeled, cored and chopped
1 tablespoon freshly chopped ginger
juice of 1 lime
3 cups chicken or vegetable stock
1 cup milk
salt and freshly ground black pepper
2–3 tablespoons crème fraîche
1 tablespoon finely chopped fresh chives

In a saucepan melt butter and add leek, celeriac, apple and ginger. Cook over a low heat for 10 minutes, stirring occasionally, until vegetables are soft. Stir in lime juice and stock and slowly bring to the boil. Simmer for 5 minutes, then remove from heat and cool a little.

Place in a food processor or blender and purée until smooth. Return to the saucepan and gently reheat. Stir in milk and season to taste. Ladle into bowls with a swirl of crème fraîche and chives for garnish.

Leek, Potato and Bacon Soup

2 tablespoons olive oil
2 medium leeks, washed and thinly sliced
3 sticks celery, thinly sliced
800 g potatoes, peeled and thinly sliced
salt and freshly ground black pepper
4 cups chicken or vegetable stock
¼ cup crème fraîche
4 slices lean bacon, roughly chopped
1 tablespoon finely chopped fresh chives

In a saucepan heat oil and add leek and celery. Cook over a gentle heat until soft. Add potato and seasoning, then pour in stock. Slowly bring to the boil and cook, covered, for 15–20 minutes until vegetables are tender. Remove from heat and cool a little.

Place in a blender and purée until smooth. Return to the saucepan and gently reheat. Stir in crème fraîche. Lightly fry or grill bacon until crisp. Ladle soup into bowls and top with crispy bacon and chives.

Cream of Parsnip Soup

25 g butter
1 large onion, finely chopped
1 leek, washed and thinly sliced
½ teaspoon sugar
½ teaspoon finely grated fresh ginger
¼ teaspoon ground turmeric
pinch of nutmeg
500 g parsnip, peeled and thinly sliced
1 medium potato, peeled and thinly sliced
3 cups chicken stock
salt and freshly ground black pepper
¼ cup yoghurt
1 tablespoon shelled pistachio nuts, chopped

In a large saucepan melt butter over a low heat and add onion, leek, sugar, ginger, turmeric and nutmeg. Cook until vegetables are soft. Add parsnip and potato and cook, covered, for a further 5 minutes over a low heat. Pour in stock and bring to the boil. Simmer for 30–40 minutes until vegetables are tender. Remove from heat and cool a little.

Place in a blender and purée until smooth. Return to the saucepan and gently reheat. Season to taste. Ladle into bowls, swirl in a little yoghurt and garnish with nuts.

Turnip and Pear Soup

2 tablespoons light olive oil
1 onion, finely chopped
3 white turnips, peeled and finely chopped
3 ripe pears, peeled, cored and finely chopped
4 cups chicken or vegetable stock
½ teaspoon lemon thyme
salt and freshly ground black pepper
1 tablespoon finely chopped fresh mint

In a saucepan heat oil and add onion, turnip and pear. Cook over a gentle heat for 3–4 minutes. Pour in stock, add lemon thyme and bring to the boil. Simmer, covered, until vegetables are tender. Remove from heat and cool a little.

Place in a blender or food processor and purée until smooth. Return to the saucepan and gently reheat. Season to taste. Ladle soup into bowls and garnish with mint.

Pear, Pea and Watercress Soup

25 g butter
1 small onion, finely chopped
500 g firm pears, peeled, cored and finely sliced
1 kg fresh peas, shelled, or 750 g frozen peas
½ cup dry sherry
¼ teaspoon salt
¼ teaspoon white pepper
pinch of ground mace
4 cups chicken stock
2 bunches watercress, stalks removed
2 dried pears, thinly sliced

In a large saucepan melt butter and add onion, pear and peas. Cook for 2–3 minutes over a gentle heat. Add sherry and seasonings and cook, covered, for 20 minutes over a low heat. Add stock and watercress and bring to the boil. Simmer for 15 minutes, then remove from heat and cool a little.

Place in a blender or food processor and purée until smooth. Then sieve soup back into the saucepan. Gently reheat. Ladle into bowls and garnish with dried pear.

Spinach and Walnut Soup

25 g butter
1 onion, finely chopped
2 stalks celery, finely chopped
2 potatoes, peeled and thinly sliced
3 cups chicken stock
1–2 bunches English spinach, well washed, stalks removed and leaves shredded
pinch of nutmeg
½ cup chopped walnuts
¼ cup crème fraîche or cream
walnut halves

In a large saucepan melt butter and add onion, celery and potato. Cook for 3–4 minutes. Add stock and bring to the boil. Simmer for 20 minutes until potato is tender. Add spinach leaves to soup for last 2–3 minutes of cooking time. Remove from heat and cool a little.

Place in a blender and purée until smooth. Return to the saucepan and gently reheat. Season to taste. Stir in walnuts. Stir in crème fraîche just before serving. Ladle into bowls and garnish with walnut halves.

Creamy Onion and Garlic Soup with Feta Cheese

25 g butter
1 tablespoon oil
2 large onions, thinly sliced
4 cloves garlic, finely chopped
2 tablespoons plain flour
3 cups beef stock
175 ml dry white wine
125 ml cream or milk
salt and freshly ground black pepper
1 cup croutons
125 g mild feta cheese, crumbled

In a saucepan heat butter and oil and add onion and garlic. Cook over a gentle heat until soft, stirring occasionally, being careful not to let them brown. Stir in flour and cook for 2 minutes, then slowly pour in stock and wine. Continue stirring until soup comes to the boil. Simmer for 15–20 minutes until slightly thickened. Remove from heat and cool a little.

Place in a blender or food processor and purée until smooth. Return to the saucepan and gently reheat. Stir in cream and season to taste. Ladle into bowls and garnish with croutons and feta cheese.

Onion and Potato Soup

20 g butter
2 onions, finely chopped
1 large potato, peeled and thinly sliced
1½ cups milk
1 bay leaf
2 cups vegetable stock
salt and freshly ground black pepper
½ cup crème fraîche
1 tablespoon freshly chopped garlic chives

In a saucepan melt butter and add onion. Cook over a gentle heat until soft. Add potato, milk, bay leaf and vegetable stock. Bring to the boil and simmer, covered, until potato is tender. Remove from heat and cool a little.

Place in a blender and purée until smooth. Return to the saucepan and gently reheat. Stir in crème fraîche. Ladle into soup bowls and garnish with garlic chives.

Pumpkin and Orange Soup

20 g butter
1 large onion, finely chopped
500 g butternut pumpkin, peeled and finely chopped
4 cups chicken stock
zest and juice of 1 orange
salt and freshly ground black pepper
2 tablespoons finely chopped fresh parsley

In a large saucepan melt butter over a low heat and add onion and pumpkin. Cook for 2–3 minutes, then add stock and orange zest. Bring to the boil and simmer, covered, for 20–30 minutes until pumpkin is tender. Remove from heat and cool a little.

Place in a food processor or blender and purée until smooth. Add orange juice and season to taste. Return to the saucepan and gently reheat. Ladle into bowls and garnish with parsley.

Spicy Pumpkin Soup

20 g butter
1 large onion, finely chopped
2 cloves garlic, crushed
1 tablespoon finely grated fresh ginger
½ teaspoon turmeric
500 g butternut pumpkin, peeled and thinly sliced
3 cups chicken stock
½ cup coconut cream
1 tablespoon sweet chilli sauce
1 teaspoon grated lemon zest
salt and freshly ground black pepper
1 tablespoon shredded coconut

In a large saucepan melt butter over a low heat and add onion, garlic, ginger, turmeric and pumpkin. Cook for 2–3 minutes, then add stock and bring to the boil. Simmer, covered, for 20–30 minutes until pumpkin is tender. Remove from heat and cool a little.

Place in a food processor or blender and purée until smooth. Return to the saucepan and gently reheat. Stir in coconut cream, sweet chilli sauce and lemon zest. Season to taste. Ladle into bowls and garnish with coconut.

hearty vegetable soups

Vegetable Soup with Olive Tapenade Crostini

?

1 tablespoon olive oil
2 parsnips, peeled and cut into small chunks
1 leek, washed and thinly sliced
2 sticks celery, thinly sliced
2 cloves garlic, crushed
4 cups chicken stock
4 potatoes, peeled and cut into small chunks
2 tablespoons tomato paste
200 g freshly shelled or frozen broad beans
100 g dried angel's hair pasta, broken into 10 cm pieces
½ cup black olive tapenade
4 slices ciabatta, grilled
2 tomatoes, finely chopped

In a large saucepan heat oil and cook parsnip, leek, celery and garlic over a gentle heat for 6–8 minutes, stirring occasionally. Add stock, potato and tomato paste and bring to the boil. Simmer gently for 30 minutes until potato is just tender.

Add beans and pasta. Cook for 10–15 minutes until pasta is tender. Stir in 2 tablespoons of the olive tapenade.

Spread remaining tapenade over crostini and spoon over tomatoes. Ladle soup into deep bowls and float crostini on top.

Moroccan Lentil Soup with Harissa

1 tablespoon olive oil
2 large onions, finely chopped
2 medium carrots, peeled and finely chopped
3 cloves garlic, finely chopped
1 teaspoon sweet paprika
1 teaspoon ground cumin
3 cups chicken or vegetable stock
2 cups green lentils, washed and picked over
½ teaspoon harissa (optional)
salt
¼ teaspoon freshly ground black pepper
2 tablespoons finely chopped fresh mint
1 tablespoon lemon juice
extra harissa
lemon wedges

Harissa
1 whole head garlic, skin removed
250 g fresh chillies
3 tablespoons finely chopped fresh mint
3 tablespoons finely chopped fresh coriander
1 tablespoon salt
1–2 tablespoons olive oil

To make harissa, place all ingredients in a food processor and blend to a paste. Add extra oil if needed to help blend the mixture. Set aside. (Place any unused harissa in a sterilised jar, pour over a little oil to cover, then seal tightly. Harissa will keep for several months in the refrigerator.)

Heat oil in a large saucepan and sauté onion, carrot and garlic with spices. Cook for about 4–6 minutes until vegetables are soft. Add stock, lentils, harissa, salt and pepper and bring to the boil. Simmer, uncovered, for about 45 minutes until lentils are tender.

Remove from heat and stir in mint and lemon juice. Serve immediately with extra harissa to taste and a squeeze of lemon.

Roasted Vegetable Soup with Lentils

2 tablespoons virgin olive oil
1 large eggplant, cut into small pieces
1 large red pepper, seeded and cut into small pieces
1 green or yellow pepper, seeded and cut into small pieces
1 Spanish onion, roughly chopped
6 cloves garlic, crushed
2 cups vegetable stock
400 g tinned tomatoes, roughly chopped
400 g tinned brown lentils
1 tablespoon ground cumin
salt and freshly ground black pepper
½ cup yoghurt

Preheat oven to 220°C. Pour oil into a shallow baking dish and heat in oven. When hot, place eggplant, pepper, onion and garlic in baking dish and baste with oil. Roast for 20 minutes until lightly browned and tender.

Meanwhile in a saucepan heat stock and add tomato, lentils and cumin. Remove cooked vegetables from oven and add to saucepan. Stir and season to taste. Ladle soup into bowls and spoon in a little yoghurt for garnish.

Lentil and Tomato Soup with Feta Cheese

2 tablespoons light olive oil
1 large onion, finely chopped
4 large tomatoes, roughly chopped
100 g brown lentils, washed
2 cups tomato juice
3 cups vegetable stock
½ teaspoon dried thyme
salt and freshly ground black pepper
40 g feta cheese, roughly chopped

In a saucepan heat oil and add onion. Cook over a gentle heat until soft. Add tomato, lentils, tomato juice, stock and seasonings. Slowly bring to the boil. Simmer, covered, for about 30 minutes until lentils are tender. Season to taste. Ladle into bowls and garnish with feta cheese.

Indian Spiced Red Lentil Soup

?

30 g butter
1 onion, finely chopped
3 cloves garlic, finely chopped
1 tablespoon finely grated fresh ginger
½ teaspoon chilli flakes
½ teaspoon turmeric
½ teaspoon coriander
½ teaspoon cumin
2 carrots, peeled and chopped into small chunks
2 cups tinned tomatoes, roughly chopped
1 cup red lentils
3 cups vegetable stock
salt and freshly ground black pepper
¼ cup creamy yoghurt
1 tablespoon finely chopped fresh mint

In a saucepan melt butter and add onion, garlic, ginger and spices. Cook over a medium heat until onion is soft. Add carrot, tomato, lentils and stock. Slowly bring to the boil. Cover the pan and gently simmer for about 40 minutes or until lentils are tender. Season to taste. Ladle into soup bowls and spoon over a little yoghurt and mint for garnish.

Spinach and Lentil Soup with Sesame Seeds

1 cup dried brown lentils, rinsed
4 cups chicken or vegetable stock
1 tablespoon sesame oil
1 large Spanish onion, finely chopped
1 stick celery, thinly sliced
1 small carrot, peeled and thinly sliced
2 cloves garlic, crushed
1 teaspoon freshly grated ginger
1 bunch English spinach, washed, stalks removed and leaves roughly chopped
2 tablespoons soy sauce
salt and freshly ground black pepper
2 tablespoons sesame seeds, lightly toasted

Place lentils and stock in a saucepan and bring to the boil. Simmer, covered, for about 35–40 minutes until tender.

Meanwhile, heat oil in a saucepan and cook onion, celery, carrot, garlic and ginger over a high heat until vegetables are lightly browned. Pour in lentils and stock and stir for 2–3 minutes. Add spinach and soy sauce and season to taste. Stir over medium heat until spinach is wilted, about 1–2 minutes. Ladle into bowls and garnish with sesame seeds.

Mexican Bean Soup with Tomato Salsa

2 tablespoons light olive oil
2 onions, finely chopped
3 cloves garlic, finely chopped
1 teaspoon ground cumin
1 teaspoon ground coriander
2 cups black or red kidney beans
6 cups water
3 tomatoes, roughly chopped
1 teaspoon salt
salt and freshly ground black pepper

Tomato Salsa
1 Spanish onion, finely chopped
250 g cherry tomatoes, roughly chopped
1 small red or green chilli, seeded and thinly sliced
6 sun-dried tomatoes, drained and thinly sliced
½ teaspoon salt
2 tablespoons finely chopped fresh coriander

To make tomato salsa, mix all ingredients together in a bowl. Set aside until ready to use.

In a large saucepan heat oil and add onion, garlic, cumin and coriander. Cook over a low heat until soft. Add beans and water. Slowly bring to the boil and cook for about 1 hour at a low simmer or until beans are tender. Stir in tomato and salt. Remove from heat and cool a little.

Place 2 cups of the soup in a blender or food processor and purée. Return to the pan, season to taste and gently heat soup through. Ladle into soup bowls and spoon over a little tomato salsa.

Rustic White Bean and Leek Soup

2 tablespoons olive oil
2 large leeks, washed and thinly sliced
4 cloves garlic, finely chopped
¼ teaspoon dried tarragon
2 cups chicken stock
2 cups tinned white beans (borlotti or cannellini)
1 cup milk
salt and freshly ground black pepper
2 tablespoons fresh lemon juice
2 tablespoons finely chopped fresh parsley

In a saucepan heat oil and add leek, garlic and tarragon. Cook for 4–5 minutes over a medium heat until leek is soft. Pour in stock and bring to the boil. Simmer for 5–6 minutes.

Place beans and 1 cup of hot stock in a food processor and purée. Return to the pan and stir in milk. Gently reheat and cook for 3–4 minutes. Season to taste and stir in lemon juice. Ladle soup into bowls and garnish with parsley.

Italian Chickpea and Pasta Soup

2 tablespoons virgin olive oil
1 onion, finely chopped
2 cloves garlic, finely chopped
½ teaspoon dried thyme
1 cup tinned tomatoes, drained and chopped
3 cups vegetable stock
1 cup tinned chickpeas, drained
½ cup orzo pasta (rice pasta or soup pasta)
½ cup freshly chopped parsley
½ cup freshly grated parmesan cheese

In a saucepan heat oil and add onion, garlic and thyme. Cook over a gentle heat until onion is soft. Add tomato and cook for 4–5 minutes until mixture has thickened and reduced a little. Stir in stock and chickpeas. Bring to the boil and simmer for 5 minutes. Remove from heat and cool a little.

Place half the soup in a food processor or blender and purée. Return to the saucepan and gently reheat. Stir in pasta and cook for 5 minutes until tender. Season to taste. Stir in parsley and ladle soup into bowls. Garnish with a sprinkling of parmesan cheese.

Eggplant and Chickpea Soup

2 tablespoons olive oil
1 large onion, finely chopped
1 large eggplant, cut into small cubes
2 large tomatoes, roughly chopped
¼ teaspoon cinnamon
¼ teaspoon allspice
1 tablespoon paprika
4 cups chicken or vegetable stock
1 cup cooked chickpeas
salt and freshly ground black pepper
¼ cup yoghurt
1 tablespoon freshly chopped mint

In a saucepan heat oil and add onion. Cook over a gentle heat until soft. Add eggplant, tomato and spices and cook, stirring occasionally, for 8–10 minutes. Pour in stock and bring to the boil. Cook, covered, for about 10 minutes until eggplant is tender.

Stir in chickpeas and cook for 3–4 minutes until heated through. Season to taste. Ladle into soup bowls and garnish with spoonfuls of yoghurt and mint.

Sweet Potato and Chickpea Soup

2 tablespoons olive oil
2 large carrots, peeled and finely chopped
1 large onion, finely chopped
1 teaspoon cumin
4 cloves garlic, crushed
600 g sweet potato, peeled and finely chopped
3 cups vegetable stock
1 cup cooked chickpeas
salt and freshly ground black pepper
½ tablespoon harissa (see page 42)
4 tablespoons creamy yoghurt
extra harissa

In a large saucepan heat oil and add carrot, onion, cumin and garlic. Cook over a low heat until soft. Add sweet potato and stock and bring to the boil. Simmer, covered, for 20 minutes until vegetables are tender. Remove from heat and cool a little.

Place half the soup in a food processor or blender and purée. Return to the saucepan. Add chickpeas and season with salt and pepper. Simmer for 15 minutes, then stir in harissa. Ladle into bowls and garnish with a swirl of yoghurt and extra harissa.

Chunky Root Vegetable Soup

25 g butter
1 tablespoon light olive oil
6 medium carrots, peeled and cut into chunks
2 large onions, roughly chopped
2 large leeks, washed and thinly sliced
2 turnips, peeled and cut into small chunks
2 parsnips, peeled and cut into small chunks
1 small sweet potato, peeled cut into small chunks
1 large potato, peeled and cut into small chunks
6 cups chicken stock
½ cup cream
salt and freshly ground black pepper
2 tablespoons freshly chopped chives

In a saucepan melt butter with oil. Add carrot, onion, leek, turnip and parsnip and cook, stirring occasionally, over a gentle heat until lightly browned. Add sweet potato, potato and stock. Slowly bring to the boil and simmer, covered, for about 20 minutes or until vegetables are tender. Remove from heat and cool a little.

Place half the soup in a food processor and purée. Return to the saucepan and stir in cream. Gently reheat and season to taste. Ladle into bowls and garnish with chives.

Borscht

1 tablespoon light olive oil
100 g lean bacon, finely chopped
350 g whole raw beetroot, peeled and coarsely grated, leaves and stems shredded
2 large carrots, peeled and coarsely grated
1 large onion, finely chopped
3 sticks celery, cut into thin matchsticks
5 cups beef stock
1 tablespoon wine vinegar
salt and freshly ground black pepper
225 g tomatoes, peeled, seeded and chopped
150 ml crème fraîche
½ cup chopped dill pickles

In a large saucepan heat oil and add bacon. Cook for 3–4 minutes over a gentle heat, then add grated beetroot, carrot, onion and celery. Cook over a low heat, stirring occasionally, for 4–5 minutes. Pour in stock and vinegar and season to taste. Cover and bring to the boil.

Simmer for 30 minutes, then add tomato and beetroot leaves and stems. Simmer for a further 15 minutes until beetroot is tender. Ladle into soup bowls and garnish with crème fraîche and dill-pickled cucumber.

Potato and Pumpkin Corn Chowder

30 g butter
2 onions, finely chopped
500 g pumpkin, peeled and cut into small chunks
500 g potatoes, peeled and cut into small chunks
4 cups chicken stock
440 g tinned creamed corn
½ tablespoon Worcestershire sauce
½ cup milk
2 tablespoons finely chopped fresh chives
¼ cup crème fraîche or sour cream

In a saucepan melt butter and add onion. Cook over a gentle heat until soft. Add pumpkin, potato and stock and slowly bring to the boil. Simmer for 10–15 minutes until vegetables are just tender.

Add corn, Worcestershire sauce and milk. Heat through for 5–10 minutes and then stir in chives. Ladle into soup bowls and garnish with a little crème fraîche.

French Onion Soup

50 g butter
4 large Spanish onions, thinly sliced
1 teaspoon sugar
1 tablespoon balsamic vinegar
4 cups beef stock
1 cup red wine
salt and freshly ground black pepper
50 g Swiss cheese, coarsely grated
1 small baguette, cut into rounds and toasted

In a saucepan slowly melt butter and add onion. Cook over a very low heat, stirring occasionally, for about 30 minutes until onion is soft and lightly browned. Stir in sugar and balsamic vinegar. Cook for a further 5 minutes, then add stock and slowly bring to the boil.

Add red wine and simmer, uncovered, for 15 minutes. Season to taste. Ladle soup into bowls. Sprinkle cheese over baguette and float on top of the soup. Serve immediately.

Mushroom and Pearl Barley Soup

30 g butter
1 onion, finely chopped
2 cloves garlic, finely chopped
2 large sticks celery, finely chopped
500 g mushrooms, wiped clean and
  roughly chopped
¼ cup pearl barley
5 cups chicken stock
1 potato, peeled and roughly grated
¼ cup finely chopped fresh parsley
salt and freshly ground black pepper
flat-leaf parsley

In a saucepan melt butter and add onion, garlic, celery, mushrooms and barley. Cook over a low heat for 20 minutes until mushrooms are soft. Pour in stock and potato and bring to the boil. Simmer, covered, for 40 minutes until barley is tender and soup has thickened.

Stir in chopped parsley and season to taste. Ladle soup into bowls and garnish with parsley.

Chunky Carrot and Hazelnut Soup

2 tablespoons light olive oil or hazelnut oil
1 onion, finely chopped
4 carrots, peeled and cut into small chunks
2 teaspoons mild curry paste
4 cups chicken or vegetable stock
100 g oven-roasted hazelnuts, roughly chopped
½ cup crème fraîche
salt and freshly ground black pepper
freshly chopped chives

In a saucepan heat oil and add onion, carrot and curry paste. Cover and cook over a gentle heat for about 20 minutes until carrot is tender, stirring from time to time.

Pour in stock and bring to the boil. Simmer gently for 3–4 minutes, then stir in hazelnuts and crème fraîche. Season to taste. Ladle soup into bowls and garnish with chives.

Italian Green Vegetable Soup

4 tablespoons olive oil
2 cloves garlic, crushed
2 large Spanish onions, finely chopped
3 sticks celery, finely chopped
2 bunches asparagus, trimmed and cut into small pieces
300 g young green beans, trimmed and cut into small pieces
200 g snow peas, trimmed and cut into slivers
200 g sugar snap peas, trimmed and halved
5 cups chicken or vegetable stock
¼ cup cream
salt and freshly ground black pepper
6 very thin slices prosciutto, grilled until crispy (optional)
2 tablespoon freshly grated parmesan cheese

Heat oil in a large saucepan and gently fry garlic, onion and celery until soft. Add half the prepared vegetables and cook for 3–4 minutes. Pour in stock and season to taste. Bring to the boil and simmer, covered, for about 20 minutes.

Add remaining vegetables and cook for 2–3 minutes. Stir in cream and check seasoning. Ladle into bowls and garnish with prosciutto and parmesan cheese.

Rissoni and Green Pea Soup

20 g butter
1 carrot, peeled and finely chopped
1 onion, finely chopped
2 cloves garlic, finely chopped
4 cups chicken stock
1 cup rissoni pasta
100 g fresh or frozen peas
100 g snow peas, trimmed and roughly chopped
salt and freshly ground black pepper
freshly shaved parmesan cheese

In a saucepan heat butter and add carrot, onion and garlic. Cook over a gentle heat until soft. Pour in stock and bring to the boil. Simmer for 4–5 minutes, then add rissoni pasta. Cook for about 10–12 minutes until pasta is just tender.

Add peas and snow peas and cook until just tender. Season to taste. Ladle soup into bowls and garnish with parmesan cheese.

Hearty Minestrone with Parmesan Dumplings

?

3 tablespoons olive oil
1 onion, roughly chopped
3 carrots, peeled and cut into small chunks
1 bulb fennel, trimmed and roughly chopped
1 small red pepper, seeded and cut into strips
100 g French beans, trimmed and cut into small chunks
¼ green cabbage, finely shredded
4 cups beef stock
1 glass red wine
400 g tinned tomatoes, roughly chopped, juice reserved
2 teaspoons dried oregano
2 Italian sausages, cut into small pieces (optional)
100 g tinned kidney beans, drained
2 tablespoons roughly chopped fresh basil
salt and freshly ground black pepper
freshly grated parmesan cheese

Parmesan Dumplings

2 slices white bread, crusts removed
3 tablespoons freshly grated parmesan cheese
pinch of dry mustard powder
salt and freshly ground black pepper
1 small egg, lightly beaten

To make dumplings, blend bread into fine breadcrumbs. Stir in parmesan cheese and mustard powder and season to taste. Stir in enough egg to bind mixture. Roll into small balls and chill until ready to use.

In a saucepan heat oil and add onion. Cook over a low heat until soft. Add carrot, fennel, red pepper, French beans and cook, stirring, for 3–4 minutes. Add cabbage and cook for 5 minutes, stirring occasionally. Add stock, red wine, tomato and reserved juice and oregano. Slowly bring to the boil and simmer for 35–40 minutes until vegetables are just tender.

Stir in sausages, kidney beans and basil. Cook for 3–4 minutes and then drop in dumplings. Cook for 1–2 minutes until dumplings are firm. Season to taste. Ladle into bowls and garnish with parmesan cheese.

Spinach and Cabbage Minestrone

2 sticks celery, finely chopped
1 large onion, finely chopped
2 leeks, washed and cut into thin slices
½ cup dry white wine
6 cups chicken stock
¼ green cabbage, thinly shredded
4 zucchini, trimmed and thinly sliced
½ cup small, dried soup pasta (acini di pepe, corallini or stelline)
salt and freshly ground black pepper
1 bunch English spinach, washed, stems removed and leaves shredded
½ cup fresh basil
½ cup freshly grated parmesan cheese

In a saucepan simmer celery, onion and leek with wine over a low heat, covered, for about 8 minutes until tender. Stir from time to time. Add stock and bring to the boil. Add cabbage, zucchini and pasta and simmer for about 10 minutes until pasta is tender.

Season to taste and stir in spinach and basil. Cook for 2–3 minutes. Ladle into soup bowls and sprinkle over parmesan cheese.

Spicy Broccoli Soup

1 tablespoon olive oil
1 large onion, roughly chopped
1 clove garlic, crushed
1 tablespoon coriander
1 teaspoon ground cumin
½ teaspoon turmeric
3 cups vegetable stock
1 cup coconut milk
1 kg broccoli, broken into small florets and stems, trimmed and chopped into small pieces
2 tablespoons freshly chopped coriander
2 tablespoons mango chutney
4 cooked pappadums

In a large saucepan heat oil and cook onion and garlic for 4–5 minutes until onion is soft. Add spices and cook for 2–3 minutes. Pour in stock and coconut milk and slowly bring to the boil. Add broccoli, reduce heat and simmer for 8–10 minutes. Remove from heat and cool a little.

Place half the soup in a food processor or blender and purée. Return to the saucepan and reheat. Stir in coriander. Ladle soup into bowls and garnish with a dollop of mango chutney and cracked pappadums.

Cauliflower and Pistachio Nut Soup

2 tablespoons olive oil
1 onion, finely chopped
2 cloves garlic, finely chopped
½ medium cauliflower, roughly chopped
4 cups chicken stock
60 g shelled pistachio nuts
salt and freshly ground black pepper
freshly chopped chives

In a saucepan heat oil and add onion and garlic. Cook over a medium heat until soft. Add cauliflower and stock and bring to the boil. Simmer for 15–20 minutes until cauliflower is tender. Remove and cool a little.

Place 3 cups of soup in a food processor or blender with pistachio nuts and purée. Return to the saucepan. Season to taste. Serve immediately, garnished with chives.

seafood soups

Ocean Trout and Lemongrass Soup

4 cups fish stock
1 cup tomato juice
2 sticks lemongrass, sliced into thin rounds
1 tablespoon thinly sliced, peeled fresh ginger
1 star anise
100 g vermicelli rice noodles
4 spring onions, thinly sliced
125 g cherry tomatoes, thinly sliced
250 g ocean trout fillet, bones and skin
  removed, cut into small chunks
1 tablespoon lime juice
2 teaspoons brown sugar
⅓ cup torn basil

In a large saucepan place stock, tomato juice, lemongrass, ginger and star anise and slowly bring to the boil. Simmer for 5 minutes to infuse flavours, then strain and pour liquid back into the saucepan.

Add noodles, spring onion, cherry tomato and ocean trout. Poach fish for 2–3 minutes until just cooked. Add lime juice and sugar. Ladle into bowls and garnish with basil.

Spicy Coconut Fish Soup with Rice

1 tablespoon Thai green curry paste
1 large carrot, peeled and roughly chopped
1 large Spanish onion, finely diced
1 stick lemongrass, finely chopped
150 g pumpkin, peeled and roughly chopped
1½ cups vegetable stock
1½ cups coconut milk
1 cup jasmine rice, soaked for 10 minutes, then rinsed
1 large zucchini, roughly chopped
250 g firm fish fillets, cut into small pieces
salt and freshly ground black pepper
3 tablespoons freshly chopped coriander
coconut cream

In a large saucepan stir-fry curry paste with carrot, onion, lemongrass and pumpkin over a gentle heat for 2–3 minutes. Pour in stock and coconut milk and slowly bring to the boil. Add rice and simmer for 15–20 minutes until tender.

Add zucchini and fish. Cook for 4–5 minutes until fish is cooked. Season to taste and stir in 2 tablespoons coriander. Ladle into bowls and garnish with remaining coriander and a little coconut cream.

Catalan Fish Soup with Potatoes

?

- 1 tablespoon olive oil
- 1 large onion, finely chopped
- 3 cloves garlic, crushed
- 2 sticks celery, finely chopped
- 1 tablespoon sweet paprika
- 1 teaspoon ground cumin
- 3 cups fish stock
- good pinch of saffron
- 1 cup white wine
- 2 bay leaves
- 400 g potatoes, peeled and cut into small chunks
- 400 g tinned peeled tomatoes, chopped and drained
- 8 uncooked prawns, peeled and de-veined
- 200 g firm white fish fillets, cut into chunks
- 8 fresh black mussels, cleaned and de-bearded
- salt and freshly ground black pepper
- 2 tablespoons finely chopped fresh parsley

In a large saucepan heat oil over a low heat and gently cook onion, garlic, celery, paprika and cumin for about 4–5 minutes, stirring occasionally. Pour in stock, saffron, wine and bay leaves and bring to the boil. Add potato and tomato and simmer for 20 minutes until potato is tender. Remove from heat and cool a little.

Place one-third of soup in a food processor or blender and purée. Return to the saucepan and gently reheat. Add prawns and fish and cook for 2–3 minutes. Add mussels and cook for 2–3 minutes until they have opened. Season to taste. Ladle into bowls and garnish with parsley.

Fish Chowder

100 g lean bacon, roughly chopped
1 teaspoon olive oil
2 sticks celery, finely chopped
1 onion, finely chopped
4 cloves garlic, finely chopped
2 tablespoons tomato paste
800 g tinned tomatoes, roughly chopped
2 cups fish stock
1 cup white wine
2 bay leaves
100 g potatoes, peeled and cut into chunks
salt and freshly ground black pepper
400 g firm fish fillets, cut into pieces
16 mussels, cleaned and de-bearded
2 tablespoons finely chopped fresh parsley

In a saucepan fry bacon and oil for 2–3 minutes. Add celery, onion, garlic and tomato paste. Cook, stirring occasionally, for 6–7 minutes. Add tomato, stock, wine and bay leaves. Bring to the boil and add potato. Season well. Simmer for 10–15 minutes until potato is just tender.

Add fish and poach for 3–4 minutes. Stir in mussels and cook for 2–3 minutes until they open. Check seasoning. Ladle into large bowls and garnish with parsley.

Vietnamese Sweet and Sour Fish Soup

4 tablespoons peanut oil
½ cup Spanish onion, halved and thinly sliced
4 cups fish stock
2 cloves garlic, crushed
1 teaspoon chilli paste
1 tablespoon soft brown sugar
3 tablespoons fish sauce
2 tablespoons tamarind paste
2 tomatoes, cut into small chunks
1 cup fresh pineapple, cut into small chunks
400 g fish fillets, cut into small pieces
1 tablespoon fresh coriander
1 tablespoon roughly chopped fresh mint
1 cup bean sprouts, washed and tips trimmed

Heat oil in a wok or small frying pan until smoking. Add onion and cook for 2–3 minutes until crisp. Remove from oil and drain on kitchen paper until ready to use.

In a saucepan heat stock. Add garlic, chilli, sugar, fish sauce and tamarind paste. Simmer for 2–3 minutes, then stir in tomato and pineapple. Add fish and bring to the boil. Cook for 1–2 minutes. Stir in coriander and mint. Remove from heat and stir in bean sprouts. Ladle into bowls and garnish with fried onion.

Bouillabaisse with Rouille

2 tablespoons olive oil
2 leeks, washed and finely chopped
1 carrot, peeled and finely chopped
4 cloves garlic, finely chopped
1 bulb fennel, trimmed and finely chopped
400 g tinned tomatoes, drained and chopped
good pinch of saffron, soaked in ¼ cup boiling water for 5 minutes
6 cups fish stock
1 teaspoon grated orange zest
salt and freshly ground black pepper
1 kg fresh seafood (a mixture of fish fillets, cut into bite-size pieces – red mullet; John Dory; flake; snapper; uncooked prawns, peeled and cleaned; mussels; clams)

Rouille

½ cup fresh breadcrumbs
¼ cup cold water
10 cloves garlic, finely chopped
6 tablespoons virgin olive oil
salt and freshly ground black pepper
dash of Tabasco sauce

To make rouille, soak breadcrumbs in water for 2–3 minutes. Squeeze dry and place in a small blender and mix with garlic (you could also use a pestle and mortar). Slowly add oil until mixture thickens. Season to taste and add Tabasco sauce.

To make bouillabaisse, heat oil in a large saucepan and add leek, carrot, garlic and fennel. Cook, stirring over a gentle heat, for 8–10 minutes until soft. Stir in tomato, saffron, stock and orange zest. Bring to the boil and simmer for 30 minutes until reduced a little and then season to taste.

Add fish in order of cooking times – thickest pieces first (about 6 minutes), delicate fish, prawns and mussels last (about 4 minutes). Ladle into soup bowls and garnish each with a little rouille.

Seafood Broth with Fish Dumplings

4 cups fish stock
2 small carrots, peeled and cut into
  thin matchstick slices
1 large leek, washed and cut into
  thin matchstick slices
1 small bulb fennel, trimmed and cut into
  small pieces
2 star anise
½ teaspoon finely grated fresh ginger
½ cup dry white wine
2 spring onions, cut into thin strips

Fish Dumplings
300 g redfish fillets
½ teaspoon salt
½ teaspoon freshly ground black pepper
1 spring onion, finely chopped
1 clove garlic, finely chopped
1 tablespoon finely chopped fresh parsley
½ teaspoon grated lemon zest
juice of 1 lemon

To make dumplings, place fish, salt, pepper, spring onion, garlic, parsley and lemon zest in a food processor and blend. Pour in lemon juice and blend to a fine paste. Remove mixture to a bowl. With wet hands roll mixture into walnut-sized shapes. Chill until ready to use.

In a saucepan bring stock to the boil and then simmer. Add all ingredients except spring onion and cook for 5 minutes. Add fish dumplings and cook for a further 2–3 minutes. Remove star anise. Ladle soup into bowls and garnish with spring onion.

Sweet Potato and Spinach Soup with Moroccan Fish Dumplings

20 g butter
1 carrot, peeled and finely chopped
1 leek, washed and finely chopped
1 clove garlic, crushed
2 teaspoons freshly grated ginger
1 teaspoon ground cumin
½ teaspoon turmeric
1 white sweet potato, peeled and chopped
4 cups vegetable stock
100 g English spinach leaves, washed, trimmed and roughly chopped
salt and freshly ground black pepper
juice of 1 lime
freshly chopped chives

Fish Dumplings

200 g ocean trout fillets, skin and bones removed or redfish fillets
1 tablespoon freshly chopped parsley
1 tablespoon freshly chopped chives
2 teaspoons freshly grated ginger
1 clove garlic, crushed
2 tablespoons lemon juice
1 teaspoon lemon zest

To make dumplings, blend all ingredients in a food processor to a fine paste. Remove and shape into walnut-sized balls. Chill until ready to use.

In a saucepan heat butter and add carrot, leek, garlic, ginger and spices. Cook for about 10 minutes over a gentle heat, stirring occasionally, until vegetables are soft. Add sweet potato and stock and bring to the boil. Cover and simmer for 20 minutes until sweet potato is tender.

Stir in spinach and fish dumplings and cook for 2–3 minutes. Season to taste and stir in lime juice. Ladle soup into bowls and garnish with chives.

Prawn and Fresh Corn Chowder

20 g butter
1 leek, washed and thinly sliced
1 large sweet potato, peeled and cut into small chunks
kernels from 3 cobs corn
125 ml white wine
4 cups vegetable stock
salt and freshly ground black pepper
125 ml crème fraîche
200 g uncooked prawns, peeled and de-veined
1–2 tablespoons lime juice
3 tablespoons roughly chopped coriander
sprigs of coriander

In a saucepan melt butter and add leek, sweet potato and corn. Cook over a gentle heat for 5–8 minutes, stirring occasionally. Pour in stock and season to taste. Bring to the boil and simmer for 15–20 minutes until vegetables are tender. Remove from heat and cool a little.

Place half the soup in a food processor or blender and purée. Return to the saucepan and stir in crème fraîche and prawns. Gently reheat for 2–3 minutes, then stir in lime juice and coriander. Ladle into bowls and garnish with coriander.

Thai Prawn and Pumpkin Soup

2 tablespoons fresh lime juice
1 kg pumpkin, peeled and cut into small chunks
½ tablespoon light olive oil
½ tablespoon Thai red curry paste
1 Spanish onion, finely chopped
1 stick lemongrass, finely chopped
3 cups vegetable stock
12 uncooked prawns, peeled and de-veined
1 cup coconut milk
1 tablespoon fish sauce
½ cup fresh basil

Pour lime juice over pumpkin and set aside. In a saucepan heat oil and add curry paste, onion and lemongrass and cook over a gentle heat for 3–4 minutes. Pour in stock and add pumpkin and lime juice. Slowly bring to the boil and simmer, covered, for 20 minutes until pumpkin is tender.

Add prawns and stir in coconut milk and fish sauce. Simmer for 2–3 minutes until prawns are cooked. Ladle soup into bowls, evenly distributing prawns, and garnish with fresh basil.

Cajun Prawn Gumbo

¼ cup olive oil
20 g plain flour
4 cloves garlic, finely chopped
1 onion, finely chopped
2 sticks celery, finely chopped
1 red pepper, seeded and finely chopped
1 green pepper, seeded and finely chopped
6 spring onions, finely chopped
4 cups fish stock
800 g tinned tomatoes, drained and chopped
2 bay leaves
1 teaspoon dried oregano
2 teaspoons dried thyme
1 teaspoon allspice
1 teaspoon sweet paprika
1 tablespoon Gumbo filé powder (optional)
1 kg uncooked prawns, peeled and de-veined
salt and freshly ground black pepper
good dash of Tabasco sauce
juice of 1 lime
2 cups cooked rice

Heat the oil in a large saucepan and stir in flour. Cook, stirring, over a gentle heat for about 10–15 minutes, until flour is a reddish brown. Stir in vegetables and cook over a low heat for 5–6 minutes. Slowly stir in stock and add tomato, herbs and spices. Bring to the boil, then simmer for 20 minutes.

Stir in prawns and poach for 3–4 minutes until cooked. Season to taste and add Tabasco sauce and lime juice. Spoon about ¼ cup of rice into each bowl and ladle soup over rice.

Prawn and Cannellini Bean Soup

1 cup dried cannellini beans, soaked in cold water overnight
2 sticks celery, coarsely chopped
1 onion, finely chopped
1 carrot, peeled and coarsely chopped
3 cloves garlic, crushed
4 cups vegetable stock
2 bay leaves
1 cup tomato purée
salt and freshly ground black pepper
12 uncooked prawns, peeled and de-veined
1 tablespoon finely chopped flat-leaf parsley

Drain cannellini beans and place in a saucepan with celery, onion, carrot, garlic, stock and bay leaves. Bring to the boil and simmer for 45 minutes or until beans are tender. Remove from heat and cool a little. Remove bay leaves. Ladle half the beans and vegetables into a food processor or blender, add tomato purée and blend until smooth.

Return to the saucepan and gently reheat. Season to taste. Add prawns and poach for 5–6 minutes until prawns are just cooked. Ladle soup into bowls and garnish with parsley.

Mussel Soup with Coriander and Lemon

1 tablespoon olive oil
1 onion, finely chopped
3 cloves garlic, finely chopped
1 teaspoon ground cumin
1 teaspoon ground coriander
2 cups fish stock
1 cup white wine
400 g ripe tomatoes, coarsely chopped
1 kg black mussels, scrubbed and de-bearded
2 tablespoons finely chopped fresh coriander
1 tablespoon finely chopped fresh garlic chives
2 teaspoons finely grated lemon zest

In a large saucepan heat oil and add onion, garlic, cumin and coriander. Cook over a gentle heat until onion is soft. Pour in stock and wine and add tomato. Slowly bring to the boil. Simmer for 10 minutes.

Add mussels. Cover and cook for 5–6 minutes until mussels have opened. Discard any that do not open. Combine herbs and lemon zest. Ladle soup into bowls and sprinkle over mixed herbs.

Scallop and Jerusalem Artichoke Soup

1 kg Jerusalem artichokes, scrubbed clean and thinly sliced
4 cups chicken stock
pinch of nutmeg
salt and freshly ground black pepper
125 ml crème fraîche or fresh cream
12 large fresh scallops
finely chopped chives

In a large saucepan place Jerusalem artichokes and stock and slowly bring to the boil. Simmer, covered, for about 30–40 minutes until artichokes are tender. Remove from heat and cool a little, then blend in a food processor or blender until smooth. Return to the saucepan and gently reheat. Add nutmeg and season to taste. Stir in crème fraîche.

Just before serving, warm the soup bowls and put 3 scallops in each bowl. Ladle in hot soup and garnish with chives. The scallops will poach in the soup after 1–2 minutes.

warming winter soups

Lentil and Tomato Soup with Lamb Kofta

2 tablespoons oil
1 onion, finely chopped
4 tomatoes, peeled, seeded and roughly chopped
1 teaspoon ground cumin
1 teaspoon turmeric
1 teaspoon ground coriander
¼ teaspoon cinnamon
1 teaspoon chilli paste
4 cups vegetable stock
150 g red lentils
juice of 1 lime
salt and freshly ground black pepper
4 tablespoons yoghurt
½ cup fresh coriander

Lamb Kofta
500 g minced lamb
1 small onion, finely chopped
2 cloves garlic, crushed
1 egg, lightly beaten

To make lamb kofta, mix mince, onion, garlic and egg together. Shape mixture into walnut-sized balls and chill until ready to use.

In a saucepan heat oil and add onion, tomato, spices and chilli paste. Cook over a gentle heat until tomato is soft and syrupy. Add stock and lentils and bring to the boil. Simmer, covered, for 20 minutes.

Add kofta. Bring back to the boil and simmer for a further 15–20 minutes until lentils and kofta are cooked. Stir in lime juice and season to taste. Ladle into soup bowls and garnish with a dollop of yoghurt and some coriander.

Japanese Spicy Beef and Noodle Soup

250 g eye fillet of beef
2 tablespoons teriyaki sauce
500 g fresh ramen noodles
5 cups beef or chicken stock
1 tablespoon chilli sauce
1 tablespoon fish sauce
1 tablespoon dry sherry
1 tablespoon sweet soy sauce (kecap manis)
juice of 1 lime
4 red chillies, seeded and cut into thin strips
4 spring onions, finely chopped
4 sprigs fresh mint
120 g bean sprouts

Marinate beef in teriyaki sauce for 15 minutes. Boil noodles for 2–3 minutes, then drain. Heat a frying pan and cook beef for 4–5 minutes each side. Remove and cut into thin slices.

In a saucepan heat stock, chilli sauce, fish sauce, sherry and sweet soy sauce and bring to the boil. Stir in lime juice. Place equal amounts of noodles in each bowl and ladle over soup. Top with beef, chilli, mint, spring onion and bean sprouts.

Barley Soup with Chicken, Leek and Mushrooms

50 g barley
juice and zest of 1 lemon
5 cups chicken stock
1 small chicken breast, thinly sliced
25 g butter
2 leeks, washed and thinly sliced
4 large mushrooms, wiped clean and thinly sliced
½ cup white wine
salt and freshly ground black pepper
4–5 tablespoons freshly chopped parsley

Place barley, lemon juice and stock in a saucepan and slowly bring to the boil. Cover and simmer for about 40 minutes or until barley is tender. Add chicken and cook for 4–5 minutes until tender.

Meanwhile, heat butter in a frying pan and cook leek and mushroom until golden brown. Add wine to deglaze the pan, then add vegetables and liquid to soup. Season to taste. Add lemon zest and parsley and check seasoning. Ladle soup into bowls, evenly distributing chicken.

Italian Chicken and Pasta Soup

1 tablespoon olive oil
1 green pepper, seeded and finely chopped
1 onion, finely chopped
1 bulb fennel, finely chopped
3 cloves garlic, crushed
1 teaspoon crushed fennel seeds
½ tablespoon dried basil
5 cups chicken stock
300 g fresh cheese tortellini or ravioli
1 cup diced, cooked chicken
3 zucchini, coarsely chopped
2 tablespoons crème fraîche
1 tablespoon fresh basil
2–3 tablespoons freshly grated
parmesan cheese

In a saucepan heat oil and add pepper, onion, fennel, garlic, fennel seeds and dried basil. Cook over a low heat, for 10–15 minutes until vegetables are soft. Pour in stock and bring to the boil. Simmer for 5–10 minutes.

Bring back to the boil, then add tortellini and zucchini. Boil for a further 10–15 minutes until pasta is cooked. Stir in crème fraîche and fresh basil. Ladle into bowls and garnish with parmesan cheese.

Chicken and Mustard Soup

20 g butter
3 leeks, washed and sliced
3 potatoes, peeled and cut into chunks
3 parsnips, peeled and cut into chunks
3 tablespoons seeded mustard
4 cups chicken stock
200 ml crème fraîche
250 g cooked chicken, shredded
2 tablespoons freshly chopped chives

In a large saucepan heat butter and cook leek over a low heat for 6–8 minutes until soft. Add potato, parsnip and 2 tablespoons of seeded mustard. Cook for 2–3 minutes, then pour in stock. Bring to the boil and simmer for 20 minutes until vegetables are tender.

Stir in crème fraîche and chicken and heat through. Ladle into bowls and garnish with remaining seeded mustard and chives.

Mexican Chicken Soup with Beans, Avocado and Tortilla

4 corn tortillas
½ cup vegetable oil
1 tablespoon olive oil
1 onion, finely chopped
1 bunch fresh coriander, finely chopped
1 small red chilli, seeded and finely chopped
2 red peppers, seeded and finely chopped
1 green pepper, seeded and finely chopped
3 cloves garlic, crushed
2 single chicken breasts
4 cups chicken stock
300 g tinned kidney beans, drained
2 large ripe avocados, peeled and stoned, cut into small cubes
juice of 1 lime

To make tortilla chips, cut tortilla into strips. Heat oil in a shallow frying pan and fry tortilla in batches, stirring gently, until crisp and golden. Remove with tongs and drain on kitchen paper.

In a saucepan heat olive oil and add onion, three-quarters of the coriander, chilli, pepper and garlic. Cook over a gentle heat for 4–5 minutes until vegetables are soft, stirring occasionally. Add chicken and 1 cup of the stock. Poach chicken for about 15 minutes until tender. Remove with tongs and shred meat with a sharp knife.

Pour remaining stock into soup and slowly bring to the boil. Stir in beans and shredded chicken to heat through. Simmer for 2–4 minutes, then stir in avocado, lime juice and remaining coriander. Season to taste. Ladle into bowl and garnish with crispy fried tortilla chips.

Mushroom Soup with Chicken Wontons

50 g dried shiitake mushrooms
1 tablespoon light olive oil
1 teaspoon sesame oil
1 large onion, finely chopped
2 sticks celery
2 cloves garlic, crushed
100 g large button mushrooms, thinly sliced
4 cups chicken stock
150 g oyster mushrooms
100 g snow peas, trimmed and cut into strips
4 spring onions, roughly chopped
¼ cup dry sherry
1 tablespoon soy sauce
finely chopped spring onion tops

Chicken Wontons
300 g minced chicken
1 teaspoon freshly grated ginger
1 tablespoon finely chopped fresh coriander
2 teaspoons soy sauce
1 teaspoon toasted sesame seeds
200 g wonton wrappers

To make wontons, mix chicken, ginger, coriander, soy sauce and sesame seeds together. Place 2 teaspoons of mixture in the centre of each wonton wrapper, brush edges with water and bring opposite points together to seal edges and make a parcel. Bring a saucepan of water to the boil and cook wontons in batches for 2–3 minutes each, then drain.

Soak shiitake mushrooms in hot water for 30 minutes, then drain. In a large saucepan heat oils and add onion, celery, garlic and button mushrooms. Cook for 5–6 minutes until soft, then add stock. Bring to the boil and simmer for 10 minutes. Remove from heat and cool a little.

Place in a blender or food processor and purée until smooth. Return to the saucepan. Add remaining ingredients except spring onion tops and bring back to the boil. Reduce to a simmer and add wontons to heat through, cooking for 5–6 minutes. Ladle into soup bowls and garnish with spring onion tops.

Spicy Chicken, Coconut and Lemon Soup

3 cups chicken stock
1 cup coconut milk
2 teaspoons lemon zest
1 large single chicken breast, cut into thin slices
1 stick lemongrass, finely chopped
4 spring onions, finely chopped
1–2 fresh or dried red chillies, seeded and thinly sliced
3 tablespoons lemon juice
2 tablespoons fish sauce
2 tablespoons coconut cream
1 tablespoon finely chopped fresh coriander

In a saucepan slowly bring stock and coconut milk to the boil. Add lemon zest and chicken. Simmer gently for 8–10 minutes until chicken is tender.

Add lemongrass, spring onion, chilli, lemon juice and fish sauce. Simmer for 1–2 minutes. Ladle into bowls, distributing the chicken evenly, and garnish with a dollop of coconut cream and some coriander.

Greek Chicken and Lemon Soup

50 g long grain rice
juice of 1 lemon
3 eggs, beaten
5 cups chicken stock
50 g cooked chicken, shredded
salt and freshly ground black pepper
2 tablespoons finely chopped fresh parsley

Cook rice for 15–20 minutes in boiling, salted water until just tender, then drain. Mix lemon juice and eggs together until well combined.

In a saucepan heat stock. Whisk about 250 ml hot stock into egg mixture, a little at a time, until combined. Remove stock from heat and slowly whisk in egg mixture. Stir in rice and chicken and cook over a low heat for 5 minutes, being careful not to let soup boil. Season to taste, then ladle into soup bowls and garnish with parsley.

Laksa with Chicken and Vegetables

?

2 cups chicken stock
250 g chicken breast fillet
2 cups coconut milk
2 tablespoons fish sauce
juice of 1 lime
500 g cooked rice noodles
125 g bean sprouts
4 bird's-eye chillies, cut into quarters
1 tablespoon fresh coriander leaves
1 spring onion, finely chopped
¼ cup fresh mint, roughly chopped

Laksa Paste
1 small red onion, finely chopped
6 cloves garlic
6 large dried chillies, seeds removed
1 stick lemongrass, finely chopped
1 tablespoon freshly grated ginger
12 macadamia nuts
4 stalks coriander, leaves removed
1 teaspoon turmeric
1 teaspoon shrimp paste
1–2 tablespoons peanut oil

To make laksa paste, place all the ingredients in a spice grinder or food processor and blend together to form a rough paste. Add a little oil or chicken stock to help blend if needed. Store in a jar until ready to use.

In a saucepan heat stock and add chicken breast. Poach over a gentle heat for 10 minutes, remove and cool. Shred chicken into strips and set aside. Add coconut milk and laksa paste to the saucepan and bring to the boil. Simmer for 15 minutes, then add fish sauce.

Place equal amounts of noodles, beans sprouts and chicken in each bowl and ladle over hot soup. Garnish with chilli, coriander, spring onion and mint.

Chicken and Corn Chowder

1 tablespoon light olive oil
1 clove garlic, crushed
1 medium onion, finely chopped
1 teaspoon freshly grated ginger
1 potato, peeled and grated
kernels from 3 cobs corn
4 cups chicken stock
2 tablespoons dry sherry
1 cooked chicken breast, shredded
1 tablespoon finely chopped spring onions
2 teaspoons light soy sauce
2 teaspoons sesame seeds, toasted

In a saucepan heat oil and add garlic, onion and ginger. Cook over a gentle heat until onion is soft. Add potato, corn and stock. Bring to the boil and simmer, uncovered, for 20 minutes until corn is tender.

Stir in sherry, chicken, spring onion and soy sauce. Cook for 4–5 minutes until chicken is heated through. Ladle soup into bowls and garnish with sesame seeds.

Chicken, Cashew and Coriander Soup

1 tablespoon olive oil
1 onion, finely chopped
1 clove garlic, finely chopped
100 g chicken tenderloins, thinly sliced
4 cups chicken stock
90 g roughly chopped fresh coriander
60 g fresh breadcrumbs
100 g cashew nuts, roughly chopped
salt and freshly ground black pepper
¼ cup coconut milk

In a saucepan heat oil and cook onion and garlic until soft. Stir in chicken and cook for 2–3 minutes. Pour in stock and slowly bring to the boil. Simmer until chicken is tender.

Add coriander, breadcrumbs and cashew nuts and cook for 3–4 minutes. Season to taste. Ladle soup into bowls and swirl in a little coconut milk for garnish.

Black-eyed Bean Soup with Chorizo

300 g chorizo, thinly sliced
1 onion, finely chopped
4 sticks celery, finely chopped
2 cloves garlic, finely chopped
500 g black-eyed beans
4 cups chicken stock
4 cups tomato juice
½ teaspoon dried thyme
2 bay leaves
3 carrots, peeled and cut into chunks
salt and freshly ground black pepper
2 cups toasted garlic croutons

In a saucepan brown chorizo over a gentle heat for 5–6 minutes, stirring all the time. Remove with a slotted spoon. Add onion, celery and garlic to the pan. (Remove some of the fat if there is more than one tablespoon.) Cook over a gentle heat for 4–5 minutes until soft. Add beans, stock, tomato juice, thyme and bay leaves and bring to the boil. Simmer, covered, stirring occasionally, for about 1 hour until beans are tender.

Stir in carrot and chorizo and cook for a further 10–15 minutes. Remove bay leaves and season well. Ladle into bowls and garnish with garlic croutons.

Transylvanian Sausage Soup

100 g lean bacon, finely chopped
1 onion, finely chopped
3 cloves garlic, crushed
500 g cabbage, coarsely shredded
1 teaspoon spicy paprika
freshly ground black pepper
800 g tinned tomatoes, roughly chopped
3 cups chicken or vegetable stock
¼ cup raisins
1 cinnamon stick
2 bay leaves
300 g Kransky sausages, cut into thin rounds
2 tablespoons freshly chopped parsley

In a large saucepan fry bacon over a gentle heat for 4–6 minutes until crisp. Add onion and garlic and cook for 4–5 minutes. Add cabbage, paprika and pepper and cook for 4–5 minutes, stirring occasionally, until cabbage is wilted. Add tomato, stock, raisins, cinnamon stick and bay leaves and bring to the boil. Simmer over a low heat for 45 minutes. Remove bay leaves and cinnamon stick. Add sausage and heat through. Ladle into bowls and garnish with parsley.

Kidney Bean and Spinach Soup with Spicy Pancetta

1 tablespoon olive oil
1 onion, finely chopped
2 cloves garlic, crushed
1 carrot, finely chopped
1 stick celery, finely chopped
kernels from 1 cob corn
2 cups kidney beans, soaked overnight
4 cups beef stock
1 bunch English spinach, washed, stems removed and leaves shredded
200 g sliced hot pancetta (spicy Italian cured ham)

In a large saucepan heat oil and gently cook onion, garlic, carrot and celery for 4–5 minutes, stirring occasionally. Add corn and drained kidney beans and pour in stock. Bring to the boil and simmer, covered, for 30 minutes or until beans are tender. Stir spinach into soup.

Meanwhile, grill pancetta until crisp. Serve soup in deep bowls with crispy pancetta broken over the top.

Spicy Bacon and Corn Soup

1 tablespoon olive oil
1 large Spanish onion, finely chopped
1 clove garlic, finely chopped
100 g lean bacon, finely chopped
1 small red chilli, seeded and finely chopped
400 g tinned tomatoes, roughly chopped
3 cups chicken stock
kernels from 3 cobs corn
½ cup freshly chopped coriander
4 tablespoons lime juice

In a saucepan heat oil and add onion, garlic and bacon. Cook over a medium heat until onion is soft and bacon lightly browned. Add chilli and tomato and cook for 2–3 minutes. Pour in stock and slowly bring to the boil.

Add corn and cook for 6–8 minutes until tender. Stir in coriander. Ladle soup into bowls and stir in a little lime juice to serve.

Hot and Sour Tofu Soup

6 dried shiitake mushrooms, soaked in boiling water for 5 minutes
5 cups chicken or vegetable stock
6 spring onions, sliced
½ cup tinned bamboo shoots, drained and thinly sliced
2 teaspoons freshly grated ginger
3 tablespoons red wine vinegar
1 small red chilli, seeded and thinly sliced
3 tablespoons cornflour mixed with 3 tablespoons water
1 large egg
1 large egg white
200 g firm tofu, cut into small chunks
1 bunch baby bok choy, leaves trimmed and sliced
3 tablespoons sweet soy sauce (kecap manis)
1 teaspoon sesame oil
2 tablespoons finely chopped fresh garlic chives

Drain mushrooms and thinly slice. Heat stock in a large saucepan and add mushroom, spring onion, bamboo shoots and ginger. Slowly bring to the boil. Simmer, covered, for 10 minutes.

Add vinegar and chilli. Stir in cornflour mixture. Mix egg and egg white together and slowly stir into soup, beating gently after each addition. Add tofu, bok choy, sweet soy sauce and sesame oil. Cook for 2 minutes, then ladle soup into bowls and garnish with garlic chives.

Yellow and Green Split Pea and Ham Soup

?

20 g butter
1 large onion, finely chopped
2 cloves garlic, finely chopped
100 g speck ham, finely chopped
1 bay leaf
½ cup yellow split peas, washed and picked over
½ cup green split peas, washed and picked over
6 cups water
1 teaspoon salt
¼ teaspoon pepper
½ cup finely chopped fresh parsley
½ cup croutons

In a saucepan melt butter and cook onion and garlic until soft. Stir in ham and cook for 2–3 minutes. Add bay leaf, split peas, water, salt and pepper. Bring to the boil and cover. Simmer for 45 minutes to 1 hour until split peas are cooked and soup has thickened.

Remove bay leaf and stir in parsley. Ladle soup into bowls and garnish with croutons.

chilled summer soups

Spicy Prawn and Cucumber Soup

1 large cucumber, peeled and seeded
salt
1½ cups tomato juice
1½ cup vegetable stock
2 cups yoghurt
½ teaspoon ground cumin
½ teaspoon ground coriander
2 cloves garlic, crushed
2 tablespoons finely chopped spring onions
1 tablespoon finely chopped fresh mint
1 small red chilli, seeded and finely chopped
salt and freshly ground black pepper
12 freshly cooked medium-sized prawns,
peeled and de-veined
extra fresh mint

Place cucumber in a sieve and lightly sprinkle with salt. Set aside. Combine tomato juice, stock, yoghurt, cumin, coriander, garlic, spring onion, mint and chilli. Season to taste.

Wash salt from cucumber and pat dry with kitchen towel. Stir into soup mixture, then stir in prawns. Chill until ready to serve, then ladle into bowls and garnish with mint.

Classic Gazpacho

1½ cups fresh white breadcrumbs
1 cup coarsely chopped fresh ripe tomatoes
1 small Spanish onion, roughly chopped
1 cup chopped cucumber, peeled and seeded
1 cup coarsely chopped red pepper, seeded
2 tablespoons olive oil
¼ cup sherry
salt and freshly ground black pepper
2 tablespoons finely chopped green pepper
2 tablespoons finely chopped red pepper
2 tablespoons finely chopped cucumber, seeded and peeled
1 tablespoon finely chopped stuffed olives
2 tablespoons finely chopped Spanish onion
½ cup croutons

Place breadcrumbs in a sieve and pour over 2 cups cold water. Drain any excess water and place in a food processor. Add tomato, onion, cucumber, red pepper, oil and sherry and blend. Season to taste. Chill until ready to serve.

In a small bowl combine finely chopped peppers and cucumber, olives and onion. Mix well. Ladle soup into bowls and garnish with vegetable mixture and croutons. Add an ice cube or two just before serving.

Spicy Andalusian Soup

1 loaf day-old white bread, crusts removed and torn into chunks
1 kg very ripe tomatoes, peeled and seeded
1 teaspoon harissa (see page 42)
2 large eggs, beaten
freshly ground black pepper
200 ml virgin olive oil
5–6 tablespoons dry sherry
2 tablespoons finely shredded prosciutto
1 cup garlic croutons

Soak bread in 3–4 cups cold water and leave for several minutes. Squeeze excess water from bread and place in a food processor with tomato, harissa, egg and pepper.

Blend together for 1–2 minutes, then slowly pour in oil until soup is a thick, mayonnaise-like consistency. Blend in sherry and season to taste. Chill before serving. Serve garnished with prosciutto and garlic croutons.

Tuscan Tomato and Basil Soup

3 tablespoons extra-virgin olive oil
1 large leek, washed and thinly sliced
2 cloves garlic, finely chopped
8 large ripe tomatoes, peeled, seeded and cut into chunks
4 thick slices ciabatta, crusts removed and cut into small chunks
½ teaspoon salt
freshly ground black pepper
pinch of sugar
20 fresh basil leaves, torn into pieces

In a saucepan heat 2 tablespoons oil and stir in leek and garlic. Cook until soft. Add tomato and cook a further 15–20 minutes until soft and pulpy.

Add bread and stir, breaking up bread as the liquid is absorbed. Season with salt and pepper and a little sugar. Cool to room temperature. Stir in basil leaves and ladle into bowls. Drizzle remaining extra-virgin olive oil over soup and season with extra black pepper.

Avocado Soup with Tomato Salsa

3 large ripe avocados, peeled and stoned
2 tablespoons lime juice
1 clove garlic, crushed
3 spring onions, finely chopped
1 teaspoon ground cumin
1 cup vegetable or chicken stock
salt and freshly ground black pepper
1 cup yoghurt

Tomato Salsa
2 firm ripe tomatoes, seeded
1 Lebanese cucumber, seeded
1 spring onion, finely chopped
1 tablespoon lime juice
½ teaspoon sweet chilli sauce
2 tablespoons finely chopped fresh coriander

Roughly chop avocados, reserving ¼ cup for tomato salsa. Place in a food processor with lime juice, garlic, spring onion, cumin and stock and purée until smooth. Season with salt and pepper. Add yoghurt and blend for 30 seconds, then chill soup until ready to serve.

To make tomato salsa, finely dice tomatoes and cucumber, then combine with reserved avocado. Stir in spring onion, lime juice, sweet chilli sauce and coriander. Ladle soup into bowls and spoon over a little tomato salsa.

Roasted Red Pepper Soup with Basil

4 large red peppers
2 cups tinned tomatoes
2 tablespoons olive oil
2 cloves garlic, finely chopped
3 cups chicken stock
salt and freshly ground black pepper
fresh basil

Slice peppers in half and remove pith and seeds. Place skin side up under a hot grill until skins blacken. Place in a plastic bag to cool for 10 minutes. Remove from the bag and peel away blackened skins. In a blender or food processor blend three of the peppers with tomatoes.

In a saucepan heat oil over a low heat and cook garlic for 3–4 minutes. Add pepper and tomato purée and stock and slowly bring to the boil. Simmer for 15 minutes, uncovered, and then remove from the heat and cool. Season with salt and pepper and chill until ready to serve.

Cut remaining pepper into thin strips. Ladle soup into serving bowls and decorate with strips of pepper and basil leaves.

Sweet Potato Vichyssoise

25 g butter
2 leeks, washed and sliced
2 large onions, roughly chopped
1½ cups chicken stock
1 cup white wine
3 red-skinned sweet potatoes, peeled and finely sliced
juice and zest of 1 lime
125 ml crème fraîche or cream
salt and freshly ground black pepper
4 tablespoons finely chopped fresh chives

In a saucepan melt butter and add leek and onion. Cook over a gentle heat until soft. Add stock, wine and kumara and slowly bring to the boil. Simmer, covered, for 15–20 minutes until kumara is tender. Remove from heat and cool a little. Place in a blender or food processor and purée until smooth. Stir in lime juice and zest and crème fraîche. Season to taste. Chill until ready to serve.

Ladle into bowls and sprinkle over chives. If soup is too thick, it can be thinned with a little more cream or chicken stock.

Leek and Almond Soup

120 g blanched almonds
2 tablespoons light olive oil
4 large leeks, washed and thinly sliced
1 carrot, thinly sliced
4 cups chicken stock
salt and freshly ground black pepper
1 tablespoon lightly browned almond flakes

Place almonds in a food processor and blend to a rough meal consistency. In a saucepan heat oil and add leek and carrot. Cook over a low heat for about 5–8 minutes until soft. Add stock and slowly bring to the boil. Simmer for 15–20 minutes until vegetables are tender. Remove from heat and cool a little.

Place in a blender or food processor and purée until smooth. Return to the saucepan. Stir in almond meal and heat through. Remove from heat and season to taste. Cool before serving. Serve chilled in soup bowls garnished with a few almond flakes.

Roasted Beetroot and Yoghurt Soup

8 medium beetroot
25 g butter
1 large onion, finely chopped
2 carrots, peeled and finely chopped
3 cups chicken stock
½ tablespoon sugar
2 tablespoons lemon juice
salt and freshly ground black pepper
1 cup yoghurt
1 tablespoon freshly chopped dill
extra creamy yoghurt

Preheat oven to 180°C. Wrap beetroot in foil and bake for 45 minutes until tender. Remove and cool. When cool enough peel and finely chop. Meanwhile, in a saucepan melt butter and cook onion and carrot over a low heat until soft. Add beetroot, stock, sugar and slowly bring to the boil. Simmer for 20–30 minutes.

Remove from heat and cool a little before blending until smooth in a food processor or blender. Stir in lemon juice and season to taste. Stir in yoghurt. Chill until ready to serve. Ladle into bowls and garnish with dill and a little creamy yoghurt.

Curried Zucchini Soup

25 g butter
1 onion, finely chopped
1 clove garlic, crushed
1 teaspoon freshly grated ginger
2 teaspoons curry powder
½ teaspoon ground coriander
½ teaspoon ground cumin
500 g zucchini, trimmed and roughly chopped
2 cups chicken stock
150 ml buttermilk
fresh coriander
yoghurt

In a large saucepan melt butter and add onion, garlic, ginger, curry powder, coriander and cumin and cook over a gentle heat for 3–4 minutes. Add zucchini and cook for 8–10 minutes, covered, until zucchini is soft. Pour in stock and bring to the boil. Boil for 2 minutes, then remove from heat and cool a little.

Place in a food processor or blender and purée until smooth. When cold, stir in buttermilk. Chill until ready to serve. Ladle into bowls and garnish with coriander and a dollop of yoghurt.

Creamy Watercress Soup

2 bunches watercress
3 cups chicken stock
15 g butter
1 Spanish onion, finely chopped
2 tablespoons flour
2 cups milk
salt and freshly ground black pepper
½ cup chilled cream

Pick over watercress and separate leaves and stems. Reserve a few leaves for garnish. In a saucepan bring stock to the boil and add watercress stems. Cook until stock has reduced by half, then remove from heat and strain liquid into a bowl.

In a saucepan melt butter and cook onion over a low heat until soft. Add flour and cook for 2–3 minutes. Slowly pour in milk and bring to the boil. Add watercress leaves and cook for a further 2 minutes. Remove and cool a little.

Place in a food processor or blender and purée until smooth. Add reduced stock and season to taste. Chill until ready to serve. Just before serving stir in cream. Ladle into bowls and garnish with reserved watercress leaves.

Garden Pea and Lettuce Soup

1 small butter lettuce
1 cup fresh mint
25 g butter
½ bunch spring onions, finely chopped
1 teaspoon sugar
750 g fresh peas, shelled, or 500 g frozen peas
3 cups chicken stock
¼ cup cream
salt and freshly ground black pepper

Wash and finely shred lettuce, reserving 4 leaves for garnish. Shred mint, reserving 6 leaves for garnish.

In a saucepan melt butter and add spring onion. Cook over a gentle heat until soft, then stir in sugar. Add peas and stock and slowly bring to the boil. Simmer, covered, for 15–20 minutes until peas are tender. Add shredded lettuce and mint leaves and cook for a further 2–3 minutes.

Remove and cool a little. Place in a blender or food processor and purée until smooth. Stir in cream and season to taste. Chill until ready to serve. Ladle soup into bowls and garnish with reserved freshly shredded lettuce and mint.

Chilled Mint Soup with Minted Pineapple

30 g butter
30 g plain flour
5 cups chicken stock
2 bunches fresh mint, leaves trimmed and roughly chopped
salt and freshly ground black pepper
100 ml cream
½ cup finely chopped fresh pineapple
2 tablespoons extra finely chopped fresh mint
½ teaspoon white sugar

In a saucepan melt butter and stir in flour. Cook, stirring, over a gentle heat until lightly browned. Slowly pour in stock, stirring continuously. Bring to the boil and simmer for 20 minutes. Add mint and cook for a further 5 minutes. Remove from heat and cool a little.

Place in a blender or food processor and purée until smooth. Season to taste. Just before serving mix cream into soup. Combine pineapple, extra mint and sugar. Ladle soup into bowls and garnish with a spoonful of minted pineapple.

Papaya and Pineapple Soup

2 red papayas, peeled, seeded and finely chopped
2 small pineapples, peeled, cored and finely chopped
4 tablespoons fresh lime juice
2 tablespoons tequila (optional)
1 tablespoon sugar
1 small firm yellow papaya
2 tablespoons freshly chopped mint
extra mint

In a blender or food processor combine red papaya, half the pineapple, lime juice, tequila and sugar. Chill until ready to serve.

Peel and seed yellow papaya, reserving a few seeds for garnish. Chop papaya into small pieces and mix with remaining pineapple and mint.

When ready to serve ladle fruit purée into bowls and stir through chopped fruit. Garnish with a few papaya seeds and whole mint leaves.

Index